CHRIST-CENTERED HEALING OF TRAUMA

Healing a Broken Heart

SMALL GROUP STUDY GUIDE

by

Norm Wielsch

For Worldwide Distribution through Ingram

ISBN: 978-1-951648-08-4

- Scriptures quoted from English Standard Version Bible © 2019
- Sample prayers used with permission from the "Hearing
- Trauma Manual" by Sandra Sellmer-Kresten, an Elijah House teaching series (www.elijahhouse.org).

LEADERSHIP
Thoughtful, Relevant Leaders From Around The World
BOOKS

LeadershipBooks.com

AUTHOR BIO

NORM WIELSCH was a law enforcement officer for over 25 years. Sixteen of those as an undercover narcotic agent. He experienced many critical incidents during his career. In 1998, he was diagnosed with PTSD and an incurable neuro-muscular disease that caused the loss of feeling, mobility, and strength in his hands and feet. After over 30 surgeries he became addicted to opioids. Due to his sinful responses to his trauma, Norm made a series of poor decisions that landed him in federal prison. It was during the most intense trial of his life that he answered the calling of God who was calling him to minister to people who were suffering from trauma. While in prison, he obtained a master's degree in Theology, a Doctorate Degree in Christian Counseling, and a Drug and Alcohol Counseling Certificate. Norm counseled inmates, preached God's word, taught bible studies. Norm Counseled many inmates who were slaves to their sin. They experienced God's healing power and transformation through the biblical principles taught through Christ-Centered Healing process. Norm was a police academy instructor and is an expert in PTSD, police tactics, narcotic enforcement, and the first responder culture. Norm is Registered Addiction Counselor and is in the process of becoming a credentialed Chaplain.

Go to www.Christ-CenteredHealing.com or
@ChristCenteredHealing on Facebook to book Norm
for your church or other speaking event.

This is the study guide for Norm's book
Christ-Centered Healing of Trauma

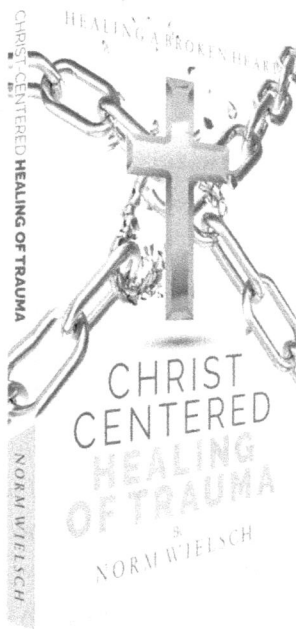

You can get a copy at:
ChristCenteredHealingBook.com

DEDICATION

I dedicate this book to my Lord and Savior Jesus Christ,

And,

To the brave men and women who protect and serve our communities, who risk their lives daily, who place the welfare of others before their own without the thought of the physical and emotional damage they may suffer.

And,

To my family who stood by me when no one else did. They endured more pain than I did during those long years I was in prison. Thank you for your unconditional love.

TABLE OF CONTENTS

STARTING A SMALL GROUP

The Christ-Centered Method of healing is a perfect topic for a small group study. A small group of friends can get together on a regular basis and follow God's principles for healing the wounds of trauma or overwhelming life events. A small group supports one another as they go through the painful process of self-evaluation and cleansing as directed by James 5:13-16. Your small group can meet at a member's home, at work, at church, coffee shop, or even at a local park. Leading a small group can be intimidating but is simply inviting some friends to get together to learn about God's will to heal -- spiritually, emotionally, and physically.

HOW TO START A SMALL GROUP

Being a small group leader requires no special training. You do not have to have any experience at all, just the will to help people by having a compassionate heart. The meeting location is flexible, anywhere there is room to meet. The only materials required is the book, *Christ-Centered Healing of Trauma: Healing a Broken Heart,* this study guide, and a bible.

SMALL GROUP TIPS

If God put it on your heart to lead a small group, don't worry, you will not have to do this alone. The Holy Spirit is there with you. God will never ask you to do something that He has not prepared you to do. When you serve God, you will be blessed. As you prepare to facilitate this small group, the following tips may be helpful to make this study a great success.

1. PRAY — It is very important to realize that you cannot do this alone. No matter how long you have been a Christian, you need the power of the Holy Spirit to complete the task. The power of prayer cannot be denied.

2. ASK A FRIEND TO HELP — Having a co-host to help and share the responsibility will make this a richer experience. Sharing this leadership role will relieve pressure and will promote spiritual maturity.

3. BE PREPARD — Obtain enough books and study guides for the group prior to the first meeting. Ask group members to read the first two chapters of *Christ-Centered Healing of Trauma: Healing a Broken Heart* prior to the first meeting. It is a good idea to read and be familiar with the material before the group meets. Have your answers to the study guide questions completed prior to the meeting. You should allow between 1 to 1.5 hours per session, once a week.

4. INVITE FRIENDS — Do not be afraid to invite friends, family, co-workers, or church members to your new group. You will be surprised how many people are living with the pain of trauma or other difficult life events. Groups can be as small as four people and as large as ten. Groups over ten people get difficult to manage. When talking to people about the group, be yourself; people will respond to your personality -- but do not push. Be a good host, be compassionate, and most of all be humble. If there is a question that you cannot answer, admit that you do not know and make an effort to

get the answer by the next group meeting. If you make a mistake — admit it. Your group will respect you and love you for your honesty.

5. GROUP AGENDA —

a) Open each meeting in prayer. Ask for a volunteer to pray out loud for the group, preferably a new member each week. Do not ask any member to pray, always ask for volunteers because some people have a fear of speaking in groups, and others may be new to the faith and are not secure in their prayers. In prayer, ask for God to open the hearts of the members present to receive the message for that day. The Holy Spirit will help you pray.

b) Ask the group if they have any praise reports. A praise report is a testimony of what God has done in the person's life. A praise report builds faith, not only for the person who received God's blessing, but also for the group members hearing about how God supports and blesses people.

c) The group leader should guide the group through the bible reading and the questions that follow. If the conversation slows or stops, ask open ended questions to keep the conversation going. As with the prayers, ask for volunteers to read the bible verses. Remember that some people read better than others so be careful not to embarrass anyone. If possible, rotate the bible verse reading through the group, everyone should get a turn. This is not only a small group study but a discipling ministry helping people to mature in the faith. Be sure to openly thank those who volunteer.

d) The volunteer should read the first question or statement, and question to be discussed. During the group discussion, it is a good idea for each member to make notes of discussion points in the appropriate space provided.

e) Do not worry about discussions that take too much time. Group discussions are very beneficial for understanding scriptures. And if the discussion leads to personal discussion of a painful event in a member's life, let it continue. The goal of this study is to heal the broken hearted, not to speed through the session. If some questions are left unanswered, have the member research them on their own time. If time allows in the next session, go over them briefly. Exposing your pain is the best medicine, let the emotions flow out. This group should be a safe place for all members.

f) At the closing of the meeting, ask if any member has a special prayer request for the group to pray about. Prayer requests can be noted in the prayer journal area to be followed up on at a later date.

g) Ask for a volunteer to close the group in prayer. Have them incorporate the prayer requests into the closing prayer. At the end, thank everyone for their participation.

6. PERSONAL JOURNEY — This is a self-paced bible study and personal growth program. Read the suggested scripture(s) or statement(s) and think about what the scriptures mean to you and how you can apply them to your life.

7. COMMUNITY — You are a member of the body of Christ. God's tool to be used in your community. It is important to spend time in Christian fellowship and serving your

community. Make an effort to take the time to complete the task.

8. MEMORY VERSE — Memorizing scripture is one method of continual sanctification. Spend some time during the week reading and praying over the assigned scripture. It is a good idea to write them on a 3" x 5" card and look at them throughout the day.

9. ROTATE RESPONSIBILITIES — One host can manage a small group effectively. But I encourage groups to rotate certain responsibilities such a prayer time, leading a discussion, refreshments, help with transportation of those in need, cleaning up after the meeting, or child care duties. Remember, ask for volunteers. Some people are unable to handle extra tasks due to their life situations. Explain to the group that serving is a commandment of God. Rotating responsibilities takes the pressure off the host and promotes growth in those who serve.

10. NEW MEMBERS — Encourage group members to recruit new people for the next group. Allow them to bring prospective members to visit one meeting to see the benefits of the study. The Holy Spirit will guide them and bring up the names of people who the Holy Spirit feels needs the study. Be led by the Holy Spirit and follow up with the names that are brought to memory. Tell the new potential member that God led you to ask them to try out the study. Have faith and remember that faith is an action word.

11. CHILD CARE — Lack of child care often prohibits many people from going to church or attending small groups. This could be a sensitive issue with some. Creativity will find solutions. You can rotate childcare duties with the

members, the group can meet in one room of a house and the children in another. Or, split the cost between the parents for a paid babysitter. The church is always a great place for small groups because they have plenty of rooms available and often have a childcare area. There may even be a teen ministry where you may get a volunteer or two to watch the kids for you.

12. GRADUATION — At the end of the 12-week study, you will have found that you have made life-long friends. You can extend one more week and have a mini graduation party. Get some refreshments and maybe even a cake. Encourage the members to bring their spouses and/or family members. The group leader could say something about the growth of each member praising them in this open format. Encourage the members to begin their own groups. God bless you as you begin this journey with your new best friends.

SMALL GROUP GUIDELINES

At the first meeting it is a good idea to make some ground rules for the group. This will ensure that all members will follow the guidelines to prevent any hurt feelings. This should be a group discussion to make sure all members agree to the guidelines. This will lay down the foundation for a healthy group experience. One member should write down each guideline as they are approved and have them typed out for the next meeting. A list of suggested guidelines may include:

- All should agree that the bible is the inerrant word of God.
- Group Attendance — Each member should make weekly group meetings a priority. Members should call the group leader if they are going to be late or unable to attend.

- Safety Zone — Meetings should be a safe place to speak freely without judgment. All should agree that anything said during the meeting will remain confidential and stays within the group.
- Respectful Discussions — All should agree to be respectful of one another. In the case of a disagreement — we agree to disagree.
- Spiritual Health — All should agree and give permission to hold each other accountable to help all group members live a spiritually balanced life by walking in the Holy Spirit.
- Building Relationships — All agree to welcome new members and to get to know all members on a personal level. All should agree to pray for one another regularly.
- No Alcohol — All should agree to make each meeting alcohol free. There is nothing wrong with small amounts of alcohol, but we do not know if a member has a problem that if alcohol is present will make them relapse. We should never do anything that may cause a Christian to fall back into sin.
- No Distractions — Group members should make every effort to avoid distractions by silencing cellular telephones and refraining from social media until the end of the meeting. Emergency situations do not apply. After the meeting it is always good to post group pictures on Facebook or other social media to plant the seed for future members.

Have the group choose any or all of these guidelines or develop your own depending on your group's unique circumstances.

GROUP LIST

1. Name _____

Phone _____

E—mail _____

Address _____

2. Name _____

Phone _____

E—mail _____

Address _____

3. Name _____

Phone _____

E—mail _____

Address _____

4. Name _____

Phone _____

E—mail _____

Address _____

5. Name _____

Phone _____

E—mail _____

Address _____

6. Name _____

Phone _____

E—mail _____

Address _____

7. Name

E — mail

Phone

Address

8. Name

E — mail

Phone

Address

9. Name

E — mail

Phone

Address

10. Name

E — mail

Phone

Address

MEETING INFORMATION

Location _____

Starting date / day / time _____

Length of meeting _____

Special assignment _____

INTRODUCTION

"The Spirit of the LORD is upon me, because the LORD has anointed me to bring good news to the poor, He has sent me to bind up the brokenhearted, to proclaim liberty to the captives, and the opening of the prison to those who are bound, to proclaim the year of the LORD's favor, and the day of vengeance of our God; to comfort all who mourn; to grant to those who mourn in Zion -- to give them a beautiful headdress, instead of ashes, the oil of gladness instead of mourning, the garment of praise instead of a faint spirit; that they may be called oaks of righteousness, the planting of the LORD, that He may be glorified."

Isaiah 61: 1-3

God sent His only Son to the earth to heal His creation; a creation that went astray when Adam and Eve sinned against Him. Ever since, we are all sinners living in an evil world, we all experience difficult times, overwhelming life events, or traumatic events. No one will go unscathed.

Some people come through difficult times without any negative effects, and some seem to be scared for life. Some never recover. Why do some of us come through fine and others seem to never be the same? Why are some held captive to the negative memories of the past and fear the future?

Trauma wounds the heart. For the purposes of this study guide I will refer to all difficult times in our lives or overwhelming life events as traumatic events. The wound of trauma is like a seed planted in your heart. For a seed to grow, it must be fed. How you feed this seed determines what type of tree will grow — healthy or sick. The bible uses agricultural terms because during that time everyone knew how to grow crops because this was their main food source. The bible speaks about the type of fruit a tree produces. This is a reference to character traits — good and bad. Good fruit is positive character traits and bad fruit is bad character traits.

If you feed this seed with anger, bitterness, and unforgiveness the seed grows into what the bible calls a bitter root. Left unchecked this bitter root will grow into a tree that produces bad fruit. This bad fruit includes selfishness, anger, hate, and depression. The root takes over your heart. Everything you do, every relationship you have will be influenced by this bitter root. Hebrews 12:15 says, "See to it that no one fails to obtain the grace of God; that no root of bitterness springs up and causes trouble, and by it many become defiled." This bitter root will not only leave you defeated but will bring pain to your relationships because of the bad fruit produced. We seem to always hurt the ones we love. Hurt people — hurt people. Other examples of bad fruit include: hate, anger, unforgiveness, resentment, frustration, and emotional unrest.

But if we feed this seed with forgiveness, understanding, compassion, and love, the seed will grow into a beautiful tree producing good fruit. In the bible good fruit is an analogy for positive character structures that exhibit contentment, peace, forgiveness, joy, compassion, and love. These character traits are conducive to a joyful life.

We can see that it is not the traumatic event that keeps us in a defeated state, it is our response to that event that causes us unrest. We all seem to respond to difficult life events in a negative sinful manner. Sin opens the door to Satan's oppression. It is through our unforgiveness, anger, hate, and bitterness that we give authority to Satan and his demons to grab a foothold in our hearts. Once allowed in, Satan will begin his oppression in our lives. Oppression is defined as a burden spiritually or emotionally; or a sense of being weighed down in body and/or mind. Sin not only gives our enemy the authority to begin his evil influence with lies, but it separates us from our Heavenly Father. Thus, we are also separated from His blessing and healing. When we repent of our sins, we restore our relationship with our creator. This restoration shuts the door to Satan and removes his ability to obtain a stronghold. Christ-Centered Healing is a discipline of self-examination, confession, repentance, and prayer that promotes sanctification. The self-examination process forces us to look at our character structures to discover Satan's strongholds in our lives. We attempt to determine the initial wound and our response to the wound. When we are honest with ourselves, we are able to identify our sinful responses to the wound. We then see the obstacles to healing that were never brought to the cross when we first received Jesus Christ as our Lord and Savior. Strongholds keep us in pain. The Christ-Centered approach destroys strongholds. Once broken, we are able to see our pain from another perspective — God's perspective. When we understand who God is and who He says we are, we can understand the truth of what Jesus did for us on the cross, our healing then begins.

Christ-Centered Healing incorporates the mind, body, and the spirit. God hates sin. God knows that unrepented sin will cause havoc in our lives. Havoc causes stress, depression, anger, bitterness which affects our physical health and can even cause disease such as heart disease, diabetes, or cancer.

God created us with emotions for a reason. Just as a physical injury to the body sends a signal of pain in that area that tells us that something is wrong, our emotions signal us a warning that something is wrong with our heart and/or spirit. Emotional pain is an indication that we are out of sync with God and that we need to realign ourselves with Him. This is done through confession and repentance. Trauma wounds the heart. Since God created our heart, He is the only one who can heal it.

I pray that this small group study brings you closer to God, opens up God's word in your heart which will bring healing, peace and joy that you never thought possible. God bless you!

Please read the first two chapters of the book prior to the first meeting.

WHY UNDERSTANDING YOUR TRAUMA OPENS THE DOOR TO HEALING

1. Members should introduce themselves
   a) Discuss and develop guidelines for the group
2. Opening prayer
3. Praise reports?

TRAUMA

4. When people talk about trauma, we first think of PTSD in combat veterans, but every person will go through some type of traumatic incident or overwhelming life event during their life. Discuss some of the events that can cause one emotional distress.

List as many as you can think of:

1.   4.

2.   5.

3.   6.

5. The result of an overwhelming life event is a broken heart. This wound is invisible but deep.

What are some of the ways people try to avoid the pain of a broken heart?

1.   4.

2.   5.

3.   6.

6. Living with the pain of a traumatic event puts us under tremendous stress due to the sinful responses we use to stop the pain. It is the sin that weighs down our heart. This stress can cause a variety of physical illnesses.

List and discuss some of the possible illnesses that stress causes.

1.   4.

2.   5.

3.   6.

7. Trauma unchecked can be written into our DNA and passed down to our descendants.

Do you have any examples of this?

_____

_____

_____

Why is it important to break this cycle of generational trauma?

_____

_____

_____

Discuss with group.

8. Prayer requests?

9. Ending prayer

PERSONAL JOURNEY

Trauma has been around for thousands of years; you are not the first to experience the pain from a traumatic event. God had a plan for the soldiers in the army who had experienced the pains of battle. In Numbers 31:19, it tells us that when the army returned from battle, they were required to stay outside the village where the people lived. The soldiers were to fellowship and pray to cleanse themselves. This spiritual cleansing is necessary for God to heal.

King David experienced trauma and wrote about it in the Psalms. Read the below Psalms and see how David found healing from God.
- Read Psalm 31:9-10
- Read Psalm 38:3-4
- Read Psalm 25:16-18
- Read Psalm 34:18

COMMUNITY

Sometime this week call a friend that you have not heard from in a long time and ask them how they are doing. Focus on them, resist the urge to talk about yourself unless you are asked. After the call, pray for them.

SUGGESTED READING ASSIGNMENT

The next six sessions will cover chapter three. Read chapter 3 in *Christ-Centered Healing of Trauma: Healing a Broken Heart* at your own pace before your next group meeting.

MEMORY VERSE

Jeremiah 29:11

"For I know the plans I have for you declares the LORD, plans for welfare and not for evil, to give you a future and a hope."

PRAYER REQUESTS:

1.   4.

2.   5.

3.   6.

SPECIAL PRAYER FOR:

1.   4.

2.   5.

3.   6.

PRAYERS THAT WERE ANSWERED:

1.   4.

2.   5.

3.   6.

SESSION TWO

WHY UNDERSTANDING THE BIBLE IS KEY TO ENSURE YOUR HEALING

1. Opening prayer

2. Praise reports?

THE BIBLE

3. The bible is the inerrant word of God. To ensure healing, we must believe that the bible is the true word of God. We cannot choose to believe one part of the bible and not another. There are many Christians and even Churches that only believe in portions of the bible, this is unhealthy. The most common doctrine that is doubted is that of creation.

Do you believe that God created the heavens, the earth, and human beings in a seven-day period?

_____

_____

_____

Discuss with the group.

4. Read Genesis 3:1-7

When Adam and Eve were in the Garden of Eden, they had everything they needed for a wonderful life. The world was a perfect place.

After they disobeyed God, what were the consequences of their sin?

_____

_____

_____

Discuss with the group.

WHO IS GOD?

5. Read Isaiah 44:6, 24-25 and 45:18; Psalm 147:3-5 & 139:1-7

List three of God's attributes:

1.

2.

3.

JESUS' HEALING

6. Read Isaiah 53:4-5

Jesus suffered greatly on the day of His death. He was beaten, humiliated, and nailed onto a wooden cross. Jesus volunteered for this torture and painful death. The punishment He endured was meant for us. Because He loved us so much, He substituted Himself in our place. Why? Because He loves us that much.

How does the fact that Jesus suffered so that you could be saved and healed make you feel?

_____

_____

_____

Does it make you want to have a deeper relationship with Him?

_____

_____

_____

Discuss with the group.

GOD'S WILL

7. Romans 12:2

What does it mean to be conformed to this world?

_____

_____

_____

Discuss with the group.

8. Prayer requests?

9. Ending prayer

PERSONAL JOURNEY

BIBLE STUDY

Read Genesis chapters 1 through 3

These chapters show a personal God, man made in the image of God, that man is sinful, Satan is our enemy, and that mankind needs a savior — a way to be forgiven. Think about what happened in the garden, and about the consequences of sin.

Do you see any similarities with how Satan tries to deceive you today?

_____

_____

_____

COMMUNITY

It is God's will to add people to the Kingdom of God. This week make an effort to talk to someone about God, the gospel, and what God has done in your life. And then invite them to your church, or the small group.

SUGGESTED READING ASSIGNMENT

Continue reading chapter three in *Christ-Centered Healing of Trauma: Healing a Broken Heart*.

MEMORY VERSE

Second Timothy 3:16-17

"All scripture is breathed out by God and profitable for teaching, for reproof, for correction, and for training in righteousness, that the man of God may be competent, equipped for every good work."

PRAYER REQUESTS:

1.   4.

2.   5.

3.   6.

SPECIAL PRAYER FOR:

1.   4.

2.   5.

3.   6.

PRAYERS THAT WERE ANSWERED:

1.   4.

2.   5.

3.   6.

SESSION THREE

WHY SURRENDERING TO GOD'S AUTHORITY WILL GUARANTEE HEALING

1. Opening Prayer

2. Praise Reports?

GOD IS SOVEREIGN

3. Read Romans 9:14-21

God is on the throne; He is in complete control of all He created. The Apostle Paul tells us that God is like a potter and His creation the clay, God thus has authority over the entire universe. After reading what Paul tells us, do you believe that we have the right to ask God why He made you the way He did?

What about the events that occur in your life?

_____

_____

_____

Have you asked God these questions?

_____

_____

_____

Discuss with the group.

GOD CHOSE YOU

4. Read Romans 8:28-30 and Ephesians 1:4-6

God is sovereign. God chose you to be saved, to live with Him in heaven for eternity. He chose you not for what you have or have not done, but because of His mercy and grace. God made the choice to provide you with salvation before He created the universe.

How does it make you feel that God chose you prior to creating the earth and everything in it and on it?

_____

_____

_____

Discuss with the group.

REGENERATION

5. Read Ezekiel 36:25-27 and Galatians 5:16-24

At the moment that you are saved, God imparts new spiritual life into you. Remember, due to the fall of Adam, we are all born spiritually dead. God gives you the gift of His Holy Spirit who lives in your heart guiding and directing you in the Christian life.

What do you think God means by replacing your heart of stone?

_____

_____

_____

Discuss with the group the fruits of the spirit, good and bad.

6. Prayer requests?

7. Ending prayer

PERSONAL JOURNEY

BIBLE STUDY

Read Romans 9:6-29 and Jeremiah 18:1-11

God is the potter and you are His molded clay. God made you the way that you are — exactly as He wanted — just as you are. If He wanted you to be taller or shorter, have a larger nose or a smaller one, He would have made you that way. You were made in His likeness — the way He wanted, God does not make mistakes, He made you with a purpose and plan in mind. You are on this earth for a reason! God's original design is that all people have the ability to make our own decisions. You have the right to decide to believe in God — or not.

Do you believe that God has the right to mold you into the person that He needs you to be in order to fulfill His plan?

_____

_____

_____

_____

_____

_____

_____

Do you believe that you should follow God's plan even when it requires you to go through a painful trial?

_____

_____

_____

Or, would you rather make your own path through life without God?

_____

_____

_____

COMMUNITY

God has a plan and purpose for your life. The bible teaches that we must love one another and care for each other, especially the less fortunate. This was Jesus' ministry. We all know that it is difficult to find the time to serve others. This is one of Satan's goals — to keep us too busy at work, at home, or even at church to serve others. Finding time to do God's will is a challenge.

Make an effort this week to find some time to help others. It could be a homeless individual who needs a meal, a neighbor who needs something fixed at home, or a church member who needs a ride to a bible study. You could help serve meals at a shelter, volunteer at a local Salvation Army Church, or donate some items to the needy. This will change your life and I believe that you will make this a regular activity.

SUGGESTED READING ASSIGNMENT

Continue your study of chapter three in *Christ-Centered Healing of Trauma: Healing a Broken Heart.*

MEMORY VERSE

Proverbs 19:21

"Many are the plans in the mind of man, but it is the purpose of the LORD that will stand."

PRAYER REQUESTS:

1.   4.

2.   5.

3.   6.

SPECIAL PRAYER FOR:

1.   4.

2.   5.

3.   6.

PRAYERS THAT WERE ANSWERED:

1.   4.

2.   5.

3.   6.

SESSION FOUR

WHAT KEY ROLE SALVATION PLAYS IN YOUR HEALING

1. Opening prayer

2. Praise reports?

JUSTIFICATION

3. Read Romans 3:22-26

Justification is an act of God, a legal declaration where God declares you "not guilty" of sin. God forgave your sins, not by anything that you have done, but by God's grace through your faith in His Son Jesus Christ. The concept of grace is very important to understand in order to live a joyful Christian life.

What does grace mean to you?

_____

_____

_____

Discuss with the group.

ADOPTION

4. Read Romans 8:14-17

You were chosen by God to be a Christian. You have been saved. You are now adopted by God to be a member of His family. You are a child of God. As a child of Cod, you are a co-heir with Jesus — you will receive an equal share of the inheritance.

What does being a co-heir mean to you?

_____

_____

_____

Discuss with the group.

SANCTIFICATION

5. Read First Thessalonians 4 :3 and 5 :23

Sanctification is an ongoing process where Christians try to live their lives free from sin. When we are born again, we become a new person in Christ. We died with Him and were resurrected with Him. Our old sinful self (old man) is dead and gone, and a new spiritual person has been born. As we mature in our faith and walk in the Holy Spirit, we are being sanctified.

What are some of the things you can do to work on your continual sanctification?

1.   4.

2.   5.

3.   6.

Discuss with the group.

6. Prayer requests?

7. Ending prayer

PERSONAL JOURNEY

BIBLE STUDY

Read Ephesians 1:3-14

According to God's will, you have been predestined to be a member of God's family — Jesus' younger brother or sister. You are now guaranteed an inheritance.

What do think your inheritance will be?

_____

_____

_____

COMMUNITY

Family and community are extremely important to God. In biblical times meals were a family affair. Family and friends would eat together and talk about their day and the scriptures. This week make an effort to eat meals together as a family. If you have no immediate family, invite a co-worker, a neighbor, a friend, or a fellow group member to have a meal with you. Sit and communicate with one another without the interruptions from the telephone or television. Try to make every meal a social event.

SUGGESTED READING ASSIGNMENT

Continue to study chapter three in *Christ-Centered Healing of Trauma: Healing a Broken Heart*.

MEMORY VERSE

Hebrews 10:10

"… we have been sanctified through the offering of the body of Jesus Christ once and for all."

PRAYER REQUESTS:

1.   4.

2.   5.

3.   6.

SPECIAL PRAYER FOR:

1.   4.

2.   5.

3.   6.

PRAYERS THAT WERE ANSWERED

1.   4.

2.   5.

3.   6.

SESSION FIVE

THE SIGNIFICANCE OF THE VIRGIN BIRTH TO OUR HEALING

1. Opening prayer

2. Praise reports?

MEANING OF THE VIRGIN BIRTH

3. Read Luke 1:26-38

Mary, a virgin, conceived a child by the power of the Holy Spirit. The birth of Jesus resulted in a human being who was fully man and fully God. Let's examine why it was necessary for Jesus to be a God/man.

a) Read Romans 3:23

b) Read Romans 6: 23

c) Read First John 2:2

d) Read Hebrews 9:22

e) Read Hebrews 10:4

f) Read Hebrews 10: 8-10

In the Old Testament or in the Mosaic Covenant, God allowed the Israelites to sacrifice an unblemished or perfect animal as a substitute for themselves to atone for their sins. This ritual was required to be done once a year. With the advent of Jesus Christ, God brought His people (Christians) a New Covenant in order to fulfill God's wrath once and for all time for the penalty for sin. God needed a perfect human sacrifice. There are no perfect human beings God is a Spirit, Jesus is also a Spirit. A Spirit cannot be sacrificed because a Spirit cannot die, God's plan was to create a perfect human being using the Virgin Mary as the vessel. The Holy Spirit caused Mary to become pregnant. This was necessary because of the requirement of a perfect human for sacrifice. The child born would be fully God (Spirit) and fully human being (flesh). A human body is able to die during the sacrifice. Jesus was that perfectly sinless human that was sacrificed for our sins, once and for all for all mankind.

4. Read Isaiah 53:4-6

Isaiah describes what the Messiah would have to go through for our salvation. The horrific pain that Jesus suffered was meant for me and you. Jesus volunteered Himself to be sacrificed in our place. That punishment was intended for us. Because Jesus was the perfect sacrifice, He took on all our sins, diseases, painful events, broken hearts, so that we would not have to bear the pain ourselves. By His sacrifice we have been healed spiritually emotionally, and physically. Our position in Christ is that we are healed!

Knowing how much Jesus suffered for you, does the forgiveness you received have a different meaning?

_____

_____

_____

Discuss with the group.

5. Prayer requests?

6. Ending prayer

PERSONAL JOURNEY

BIBLE STUDY

Read Isaiah chapters 53 and 61

In chapter 61 the Prophet Isaiah is predicting the coming of the Messiah, Jesus Christ. Chapter 61 describes Jesus' mission on earth. Chapter 53 describes the pain and suffering that the Messiah would endure for mankind's salvation. These predictions were made hundreds of years prior to the birth of Jesus. All these predictions came true.

After reading these predictions, does it help solidify your faith that the bible is the true and accurate word of God?

_____

_____

_____

Do these predictions alter your belief in who Jesus is? What He endured? And the results of His death and resurrection?

_____

_____

_____

COMMUNITY

Take a few minutes each day to pray for someone you know is going through a difficult time, or pray for someone that you know does not yet know Jesus — pray for their salvation, or pray for the safety of our first responders who place themselves in danger every day to keep your family safe.

SUGGESTED READING ASSIGNMENT

Continue your study in *Christ-Centered Healing of Trauma: Healing a Broken Heart*.

MEMORY VERSE

John 3:16

"For God so loved the world, that He gave His only Son, that whoever believes in Him should not perish but have eternal life."

PRAYER REQUESTS:

1.   4.

2.   5.

3.   6.

SPECIAL PRAYER FOR:

1.   4.

2.   5.

3.   6.

PRAYERS THAT WERE ANSWERED?

1.   4.

2.   5.

3.   6.

SESSION SIX

UNDERSTANDING HOW SIN IS THE CULPRIT THAT KEEPS US BROKEN

1. Opening prayer

2. Praise reports?

SIN

3. Read First John 1:5-10 & James 4:17

Sin is a rebellion or the disobedience of God. Sin can be knowingly committed — an act of commission, or the sin of doing or not doing something that you should have done — an act of omission. A sin can be anything that goes against God's will or moral standards. In this world that Satan controls, an activity that this "world" condones or even promotes can be a sin. When we follow God's moral standards, we are in His will.

When we sin (and we will), what must we do to be forgiven?

_____

_____

_____

In the above text it speaks of walking in darkness. What does it mean to walk in darkness?

_____

_____

_____

Discuss with the group.

SIN HAS CONSEQUENCES

4. Read Hebrews 12:5-11

God hates sin. God knows that sin will cause havoc in our lives and will eventually destroy us. This is why He must correct us when we sin — just as our parents corrected us when we did something we should not have. God disciplines us because He loves us, not because He is a mean heavenly Father. All parents know that when a child is not disciplined for poor behavior, they will later become unable to follow any moral standards. Children require discipline. It is through discipline that they grow and become better people.

What are some of the consequences of sin?

_____

_____

_____

Discuss with the group.

Read John 5:1-7 and Psalm 38:3

The bible teaches that one of the consequences of sin is emotional and/or physical illness. Because of Jesus' work on the cross, our position in Christ is "healed." In order to obtain that healing we must overcome the obstacle of unrepented sin. Once forgiven and in fellowship with God, your healing will begin.

Discuss the importance of confession and repentance.

_____

_____

_____

5. Prayer requests?

6. Ending prayer

PERSONAL JOURNEY

BIBLE STUDY

Read Second Samuel chapters 11 through 18

Take this week to read about King David and his sin. David paid a huge price for the sin he committed. While reading through the chapters, try to identify each consequence of his sin. Think about your experiences. Looking back do you think that any of your pain is a result of your sins?

COMMUNITY

This week keep your eye out for people in need. If you see someone struggling with an issue, try to help them — even if it is just a kind word. Right now, pray that the Holy Spirit places someone in your path that you can be a blessing to. Pray for wisdom and discernment for people in need. If you are worried about what to say to them, trust the Holy Spirit to give you the words to say. The body of Christ is meant to edify and help one another, this is God's will.

SUGGESTED READING ASSIGNMENT

Finish your study of chapter three in *Christ-Centered Healing of Trauma; Healing a Broken Heart.*

MEMORY VERSE

First John 1:9

"If we confess our sins, He is faithful and just to forgive us our sins, and to cleanse us from all unrighteousness."

PRAYER REQUESTS:

1.   4.

2.   5.

3.   6.

SPECIAL PRAYER FOR:

1.   4.

2.   5.

3.   6.

PRAYERS THAT WERE ANSWERED:

1.   4.

2.   5.

3.   6.

SESSION SEVEN

WHY KNOWING WHO YOU ARE IN CHRIST AFFECTS YOUR HEALING

1. Opening prayer

2. Praise reports?

WHO YOU ARE IN CHRIST?

3. You are God's workmanship. He made you exactly the way He intended. You are not who or what other people say you are, you are not your mistakes, you are not what happened to you, you are not the product of your trauma, you are not a victim. You are who God says you are — PERIOD! Understanding and believing who God says you are, is the key to living a life filled with peace and joy. You will have the contentment in all circumstances that only a loving relationship with God will provide.

Take turns reading the below scriptures in the group and discuss their meaning to you in the group.

- Ephesians 2:10
- Second Corinthians 5:17
- Colossians 3:12-18
- Philippians 4:11-13
- Romans 8.31-39
- Psalm 86:5
- Psalm 106:1
- Second Corinthians 13: 14

Satan's mission is to instill doubt in you so that you do not believe that God loves you more than you could ever comprehend. Do not believe Satan's lies. You are who God says you are — nothing less.

4. Prayer requests?

5. Ending prayer

PERSONAL JOURNEY

BIBLE STUDY

Read Second Corinthians 10:3-6

Christians are involved in a constant spiritual battle; we are engaged in spiritual warfare! The Apostle Paul tells us to take every thought captive and compare it to the Word of God. If that thought inspired by Satan is telling you that you are no good and that you do not deserve God's forgiveness, you must take that thought captive and compare it to what God says. What does God say? You are wonderfully made (Psalm 139:14) and that God's love is abounding. Does that agree with the thought you just had? NO! When you determine that your thought does not agree with what God says about you, you must reject that thought. Out loud, reaffirm who God says you are. Tell Satan that you belong to Jesus! This new thought process may be difficult at first because Satan has been lying to you for a long time and his negativity has been engrained in you from an early age. As you practice evaluating your negative thoughts, it will become habit and soon it will be natural. This will help you in your walk in the Holy Spirit and your sanctification. Promise yourself today that every negative thought will be evaluated and compared to God's word.

COMMUNITY

As you progress in your sanctification your worldview will change. The things that you once said and did, you will no longer do. These things may be cursing, negative speak, putting people down, gossip, or prideful talk.

We all use social media. There is nothing wrong with staying in touch with friends and family who share similar values, however, we all know that there is a lot of negativity on social media. It is important to not get caught up in the negativity and bullying. Starting today, make an effort to stand for positive affirmations and renounce negative talk, gossip, and bullying. As a Christian you must put out a positive message, everyone is watching what Christians do and how they act. Many people know what Christians are against, but few know what Christians stand for -- LOVE! When you see negativity call it out. Spread the word that God loves them and they are God's children -- a revival can begin with one positive post!

SUGGESTED READING ASSIGNMENT

Read Chapter 4 in *Christ-Centered Healing of Trauma: Healing a Broken Heart* before the next meeting.

MEMORY VERSE

Romans 5:8

"…but God shows His love for us in that while we were still sinners, Christ died for us."

PRAYER REQUESTS:

1.   4.

2.   5.

3.   6.

SPECIAL PRAYER FOR:

1.   4.

2.   5.

3.   6.

PRAYERS THAT WERE ANSWERED:

1.   4.

2.   5.

3.   6.

SESSION EIGHT

WHY GOD ALLOWS SUFFERING AND TRAUMA?

1. Opening prayer

2. Praise reports?

WHY GOD ALLOWS SUFFERING

3. When I talk to people about God, I find that the most common questions is, "Why does God allow suffering?" And, "Why doesn't He stop it?" This is a deep and complex question that requires much study to come close to understanding. We know that Adam gave authority to Satan to rule the earth and all that is on it. Prior to Adam's sin everything was perfect. At the fall, everything changed. Satan now rules the earth. It is Satan's goal to destroy all of God's followers. Satan wants revenge at God for kicking him out of heaven. Satan does this by causing pain and suffering in an attempt to get believers to blame God for our pain, thus forsaking God. God knows Satan's plan. He sent

Jesus to defeat Satan, this was accomplished at the cross. We are victorious. But few Christians realize the victory because they remain in habitual sin and are enslaved by their sin — Satan's goal accomplished!

Even as we resist Satan's lies, God sometimes allows or causes trials in our lives to mold us or train us to fulfill His plan and purpose for our life.

Other reason for trials in our lives include:

a) Read First Peter 4:12-13

God may use a trial in your life to test your faith

b) Read Deuteronomy 8:2

God may use a trial in your life to humble you when He believes that you have become too prideful. Pride is the root cause of most sin.

c) Read First Peter 1:6-7

God may use a trial in your life to refine you, to make you better, or to prepare you to fulfill a plan that He has for you.

d) Read John 9:3-7

God may use a trial in your life to glorify Himself — this brings others to repentance.

e) Read Second Corinthians 1:3-7

God may use a trial in your life to make you stronger, to gain wisdom and compassion that will later be used to comfort others who will go through similar trials. Your testimony can comfort others and increase their faith.

f) Read Hebrews 12: 5-11

God may use a trial in your life as a means of correction or discipline because of your sins. As you suffer the pain of discipline, you are drawn closer to God. Through times of pain you learn obedience and trust. Your relationship with God will grow, this may not happen without the trial.

4. Romans 8:28-29

No matter the reason for your trial and your pain, God will use your experience for good. Something good will come out of your pain when you love God.

Do you see God in any of the trials and pain that you have experienced?

_____

_____

_____

Discuss with the group.

5. Prayer requests?

6. Ending prayer.

PERSONAL JOURNEY

Read the story of Joseph, Genesis chapters 37 through 50

Joseph was favored by God. But Joseph was placed through many traumatic events during his young life. His brothers sold him into slavery in Egypt. He was a slave to a man named Potiphor. Potiphor's wife falsely accused him of rape. Joseph was sent to prison. Through this time in prison, God was with Joseph, as He is with us at times of trials. God had a plan. At the right time, God promoted Joseph to second in command of Egypt. Eventually Joseph confronted his brothers. Read what happens.

God used Joseph's trials to save lives — the lives of the nation of Israel. God has a plan and purpose for everyone, even you! Your trial may be used to help others that you do not even know. Christians must look at their situation from God's perspective, not a worldly perspective. When we see our pain as God does, it should comfort us to know that He is on the throne and in charge — He is with you.

COMMUNITY

Share this study with someone that you believe may be going through a difficult time.

Reassure them that God has a plan — they only need to trust.

SUGGESTED READING ASSIGNMENT

Read Chapter 8 in *Christ-Centered Healing of Trauma: Healing a Broken Heart* before the next meeting.

MEMORY VERSE

Romans 8:28

"And we know that for those who love God all things work together for good, for those who are called according to His purpose."

PRAYER REQUESTS:

1.   4.

2.   5.

3.   6.

SPECIAL PRAYER FOR:

1.   4.

2.   5.

3.   6.

PRAYERS THAT WERE ANSWERED:

1.   4.

2.   5.

3.   6.

SESSION NINE

CRITICAL OBSTACLES TO HEALING AND SPIRITUAL PRINCIPLES

1. Opening prayer

2. Praise reports?

JUDGING OTHERS

3. Read Matthew 7:1-2

Romans 2:1-3

One obstacle to our healing is the judgment of others. Judging others is a natural human trait, we tend to judge almost everyone. Jesus warns us that if we judge others our heavenly Father will judge us. Judging what others do is acceptable, however, when we judge others for who they are — we condemn them. The Apostle Paul adds that when we condemn others for who they are, this sinful judgment condemns us to do the very same things.

Discuss with the group why do you think we love to judge others and gossip about the things others do, when we do similar things.

_____

_____

_____

INNER VOWS

4. When we are wounded, we tend to make promises to ourselves to do or not to do something that we believe will protect us from further wounding and pain. Inner Vows are sinful because they enforce our will — not God's will.

Have you ever made an inner vow? If so, how did it protect you?

_____

_____

_____

Discuss with the group.

SOWING AND REAPING

5. Read Galatians 6:7-8

The law of sowing and reaping is actually a very simple spiritual law. If you do good things, good things will be returned to you. If you do bad things, bad things will be returned to you. The effects of this law are not always immediately realized, often the reaping occurs much later.

Have you experienced the results of this spiritual law?

_____

_____

_____

Now that you understand this law, how will your behavior change?

_____

_____

_____

Discuss in the group.

THE LAW OF INCREASE

6. Read Mark 4:24

This is also a very simple law. If you do good things, the good things returned to you will be increased. And if you do bad things, the bad things returned to you will be increased.

THE LAW OF DIMINISHING RETURNS

7. Humans tend to get bored easily. In reference to sin, we often get bored when we are in habitual sin. Remember unrepented sin is an obstacle to healing. The first time we commit a sin, our conscience warns us that we did something against God's moral laws. If we ignore our guilty conscience and continue in that sin, our conscience becomes calloused. We build a tolerance to the sin and our conscience stops bothering us. The more we sin, the less we feel guilt. Eventually we can even justify our sin as normal. When our conscience becomes calloused, we sometimes

step up the severity of the sin. We then stay in a cycle of pain due to the unrepented sin.

How can we prevent our conscience from building up that callous or tolerance to sin?

_____

_____

_____

If we ignore this spiritual principle, how will this affect our life in the long-term?

_____

_____

_____

Discuss with the group.

HONORING PARENTS

8. Read Ephesians 6:1-3

God commands us to honor our parents. This is a commandment with a promise. If we follow this commandment, God promises all will go well with us. We know that some parents do not deserve to be honored, but as Christians we must follow God's commandments. How might we honor our parent(s) who do not deserve "honor" because of neglect or abuse during childhood?

_____

_____

_____

Discuss with the group.

9. Prayer Requests?

10. Ending prayer.

PESONAL JOURNEY

BIBLE STUDY

Read Exodus 20:1-18 – The Ten Commandments

These are God's written laws. These are the rules we are to live by.

How do you feel about the Ten Commandments?

Do you agree the best way to fulfill the commandments is to love one another as Jesus commands?

COMMUNITY

Sometime this week call your parent(s) on the telephone and tell them how much you love them for all the things they have sacrificed for you during your youth and if necessary, forgive them for what they have done to cause you pain. If your parents are no longer alive, visit their grave or write them a letter telling them how you feel. Take this time to renounce not honoring your parents and repent for it. Restore your relationship now.

SUGGESTED READING ASSIGNMENT

For the next two weeks, we will be in chapter 8 in *Christ-Centered Healing of Trauma: Healing a Broken Heart.*

MEMORY VERSE

Galatians 6:7-8

"Do not be deceived: God is not mocked, for whatever one sows, that will he also reap. For the one who sows to his own flesh will from the flesh reap corruption, but the one who sows to the Spirit will from the Spirit reap eternal life."

PRAYER REQUESTS:

1.   4.

2.   5.

3.   6.

SPECIAL PRAYER FOR:

1.   4.

2.   5.

3.   6.

PRAYERS THAT WERE ANSWERED:

1.   4.

2.   5.

3.   6.

SESSION TEN

WHY FORGIVENESS IS CRITICAL TO HEALING

1. Opening prayer

2. Praise reports?

FORGIVENESS

3. Read Matthew 6:14 — 15

This scripture is very powerful. Jesus is telling His followers that we must forgive those who we perceived harmed us in some way. I added the word perceived because sometimes due to our excess baggage we misinterpret actions or statements by others. Because of our pain we see the world from a different perspective. The person who we believe harmed us may also becoming from a place of pain, and never meant the statement to come out in an offensive manner. We must honestly evaluate the event that we believe harmed us.

Was this meant to cause pain? Or not?

Jesus understands that unforgiveness will keep us in our pain. It is a sin to withhold forgiveness. This is why Jesus commands us to forgive those who harmed us. If you do not forgive, your heavenly Father will not forgive your sins.

Forgiving is difficult -- but necessary. What are some of the ways we can obtain the strength to forgive?

_____

_____

_____

Discuss with the group.

4. Read Matthew 18:21-22

What do you think about Jesus' teaching of forgiving others over and over again?

_____

_____

_____

5. Read Matthew 5:23-24

Jesus teaches us that when we harm someone else, we must seek their forgiveness. This is so important that Jesus tells us that we must seek forgiveness prior to prayer. This suggests that not seeking forgiveness is a sin. Therefore, if we do not ask for forgiveness of our Heavenly Father will not hear our prayer.

Seeking forgiveness is equally as difficult as forgiving others. Our pride and bitterness stands in the way of our healing. What are some of the ways we can seek out forgiveness from others?

_____

_____

_____

Discuss with the group.

6. Prayer requests?

7. Ending prayer

PERSONAL JOURNEY

BIBLE STUDY

Read Colossians 3:12-13

You have been chosen by God to be a Christian. You have been tasked to be kind, compassionate, and forgiving, as God has forgiven you.

Are you abiding in God's will by forgiving those who have offended you? If not, what can you do to get back into God's will?

COMMUNITY

Take some time this week and think about if there is anyone that you need to forgive, or anyone that you must seek forgiveness from. Write their names down. If there is someone you must speak with, reach out to them and initiate the process of forgiving or seeking forgiveness. If the person is no longer around, write them a letter forgiving them, you don't have to mail it.

SUGGESTED READING ASSIGNMENT

Read Chapter 8 and 9 in *Christ-Centered Healing of Trauma: Healing a Broken Heart* before the next meeting.

MEMORY VERSE

Ephesians 4:32

"Be kind to one another, tender-hearted, forgiving one another, as God in Christ forgave you."

PRAYER REQUESTS:

1.   4.

2.   5.

3.   6.

SPECIAL PRAYER FOR:

1.   4.

2.   5.

3.   6.

PRAYERS THAT WERE ANSWERED:

1.   4.

2.   5.

3.   6.

SESSION ELEVEN

WHY CONFESSION AND REPENTANCE ARE GATEWAYS TO HEALING

1. Opening prayer

2. Praise reports

3. Read First John 1:8-10

CONFESSION

Confession is an admission of guilt; we acknowledge we have violated God's moral standards. After confessing our sin to God, we have to repent of that sin. Repentance is a genuine remorse for that sin and then making a sincere effort to turn away from that sin. When we confess and repent, God forgives us of that sin. Unrepented sin blocks our healing.

When you realize that you have sinned, what do you do?

_____

_____

_____

Do you repent immediately or wait until church next week?

_____

_____

_____

Discuss with the group.

WALKING IN THE HOLY SPIRIT

4. Read Galatians 5:16-17

God's gift to Christians is His Holy Spirit, the Holy Spirit lives in your heart. It is God's Holy Spirit that leads us, guides us in our lives, and teaches us God's truth. When we follow the Holy Spirit, we are said to be _walking in the Spirit_. As we walk more and more in the Spirit, we are being sanctified. We are God's hands and feet to do His will here on earth.

Have you ever felt the Holy Spirit directing you to do something?

_____

_____

_____

Did you do it? Why or why not?

_____

_____

_____

Discuss with the group.

YOUR TESTIMONY

5. Read Psalms 96:2-3

Your testimony is simply your story. Your testimony is a powerful tool. God sometimes allows trials in our lives to give us a testimony so that as God helps us through the trial, we can tell others about how God helped us through. It is through your testimony that you glorify God. As you tell others your testimony, you are not only helping someone who is in their own trial, but you are fulfilling Jesus' command to spread the gospel (Acts 1:8). You will never know how your testimony will impact another's life. This maybe the seed of God placed in their heart, or it may be the turning point that brings them to repentance. Testimonies increase believer's faith and bring non-believers closer to God.

Are you prepared to give your testimony to someone who needs to hear it?

_____

_____

_____

Discuss with the group.

6. Prayer requests?

7. Closing prayer

PERSONAL JOURNEY

BIBLE STUDY

Read First Corinthians 1:26-31

God chooses people who are flawed and broken to deliver His message and to fulfill His purpose here on earth. He does not use presidents, kings, billionaires, or even social media stars to deliver His message — the gospel. All your pain, the traumatic things that you have endured, the bad decisions that you made, the loses that you have faced, the illness that you are suffering with, God will use for you to be a walking billboard to the love and mercy of God. Just as Jesus shows His puncture wounds as His testimony, you are to use your pain to glorify God. He will use your testimony to bring others to the kingdom of God. Tell everyone your story — whoever will listen. Thank God that He loves you and is with you through your trial. Pray that God will send people across your path to tell your testimony so that they can be comforted by your experiences.

COMMUNITY

Your testimony is an important part of your Christian life. It is the way we behave that sets us apart from non-believers. It is the fruit that we produce that sets an example for others.

This week pay close attention on how you act and interact with others. If someone spoke to you for five minutes would they know that you are a Christian? Do you believe that you are setting a positive example to others? Or a poor example?

SUGGESTED READING ASSIGNMENT

Read Chapter 9 in *Christ-Centered Healing of Trauma: Healing a Broken Heart*

MEMORY VERSE

1 John 1:9

"If we confess our sins, He is faithful and just to forgive us our sins and to cleanse us from all unrighteousness."

PRAYER REQUESTS:

1.   4.

2.   5.

3.   6.

SPECIAL PRAYER FOR:

1.   4.

2.   5.

3.   6.

PRAYERS THAT WERE ANSWERED:

1.   4.

2.   5.

3.   6.

SESSION TWELVE

HOW TO USE THE POWERFUL TOOL OF PRAYER TO ENERGIZE HEALING

1. Opening prayer

2. Praise reports?

3. Read Second Chronicles 7:14

Prayer is the most powerful tool in a Christian's toolbox. It is also the most underused tool. The bible teaches us to pray under all circumstances — continually. Prayer should be our first action when a decision has to be made or an overwhelming life event pops up. God tells us directly — if we humble ourselves and place Him first in our lives, we pray, and obey His simple command — love one another — we will be healed.

Do you pray when presented with a difficult decision or circumstance presents itself?

_____

_____

_____

Or, do you try to use your own understanding to get through the difficult time, asking God for help as a last resort?

_____

_____

_____

Discuss with the group.

4. A simple prayer model is "ACTS"

A -- Adoration — Praise God for who He is and what He represents

C — Confession — Confess and repent your sins

T -- Thanksgiving — Thank God for all the blessings He has provided you

S – Supplication — Ask for the things that are on your heart

This prayer model is based on the Lord's prayer in Matthew 6:5-15. This is a good guideline to follow. Prayer is just a communication with your heavenly Father, any style is permissible. Any conversation with God is good.

What is your style of prayer?

_____

_____

_____

Have each group member provide their style.

5. Read James 4:2-3 & First John 5:14-15

When we pray with requests, we must understand that for the prayer to come to pass it must be in God's will. Prayer is powerful (James 5: 16), prayer may just change God's mind. The bible does teach that God may change His mind based on repentance and prayer.

How can we know God's will?

1.   4.

2.   5.

3.   6.

Discuss with the group.

6. Prayer requests?

7. Ending prayer

PERSONAL JOURNEY

BIBLE STUDY

Read Matthew 17:14-21

Fasting is another powerful tool. Fasting supercharges prayer. Jesus tells His disciples that the boy possessed a demon that was so powerful that the demon could only be removed by prayer with fasting. The Israelites used fasting to cleanse their sins, regain lost holiness, and to receive God's blessing. Jesus used fasting in spiritual warfare. Fasting must be done with a humble heart for the proper reasons. Fasting will bring you closer to God.

COMMUNITY

Consider a group service project. Discuss a way for the entire group to serve the community together. Some activities to consider could be:

- Make sack lunches to hand out to the homeless
- Ask your church if they need some maintenance like weeding, painting, or cleaning
- Serve together at the Salvation Army or another ministry that serves the needy
- Choose a local park or school that needs clean up or playground repair.

SUGGESTED READING ASSIGNMENT

Read through the APPENDIX of Prayers in *Christ-Centered Healing of Trauma: Healing a Broken Heart.* Use any sample prayer that applies to your needs.

MEMORY VERSE

James 5:16

"Therefore, confess your sins to one another, that you may be healed. The prayer of a righteous person has great power as it is working."

PRAYER REQUESTS:

1.   4.

2.   5.

3.   6.

SPECIAL PRAYER FOR:

1.   4.

2.   5.

3.   6.

PRAYERS THAT WERE ANSWERED:

1.   4.

2.   5.

3.   6.

CONGRATULATIONS!

You have completed this small group study on Christ-Centered Healing. I pray that this study has been a blessing to you and that you are able to take something away from the study and group discussions.

The goal of this study was to make you aware of the obstacles that prevent healing. Hopefully we have shown you how to overcome the obstacles in your life that prevent your healing and how to restore your relationship with God. In God's Will there is healing,

If any aspect of the book *Christ-Centered Healing of Trauma: Healing a Broken Heart* or this study guide has blessed you, please send us an email at: info@Christ-CenteredHealing.com. Tell us your story! Remember, your testimony is powerful! Check us out on Facebook (@ChristCenteredHealing) and on Instagram and Twitter. Thank you for sharing your journey with group.

We encourage you to have one more meeting together and celebrate what God has done in your lives through this small group study. Plan a group dinner, picnic, barbecue, or any other get together to praise God. This would be a good time to invite friends, family, co-workers, potential new members, and even those who have not yet come to have a relationship with Jesus. Celebrate God's blessings.

SCRIPTURES RELATING TO TRANSFORMATION

Romans 12:1-2
Ephesians 4:22-24
Colossians 3:5-10
Second Corinthians 4:16
Philippians 1:6

SCRIPTURES RELATED TO HEALING

Psalm 51:10-12
Psalm 139:13-16 and 23-24
Psalm 10:14
Psalm 68:5-6
Psalm 82:3
Psalm 146:9
Hosea 14:3

SCRIPTURES RELATING TO ABANDONMENT

Isaiah 53:4-5 Isaiah 57:18
Ezekiel 11:19
Luke 4: 18
Luke 6:17-8 and 8:31

THIS POEM SHOWS THE TRUTH OF GOD'S LOVE

FOOTPRINTS

One night I had a dream, I dreamed I was walking along the beach with the Lord. Across the sky flashed scenes from my life. For each scene, I noticed two sets of footprints in the sand; one belonging to me, and the other to the Lord.

When the last scene of my life flashed before me, I looked back at the footprints in the sand, I noticed that many times along the path of my life there was only one set of footprints, I also noticed that it happened at the very lowest and saddest times in my life.

This really bothered me and I questioned the Lord about it, "Lord, you said that once I decided to follow You. You'd walk with me all the way. But I have noticed that during the most troublesome times in my life, there is only one set of footprints. I don't understand why when I needed You most you would leave me."

The Lord replied, "My precious, precious child, I love you and I would never leave you. During your times of trial and suffering, when you see only one set of footprints, it was then that I carried you."

Unknown author — obtained from the Salvation Army Correctional Services

NORM'S SESSION NOTES

Healing of trauma is based on your relationship with God. To begin the healing process, you must understand who God is and who you are in Christ. This can only be done through learning and understanding the Word of God. This small group guide will help you in your journey through the Christ-Centered Healing process. Group discussion is extremely important in gaining understanding in the human condition. Each member will learn something from other members. Norm has made the below notes for each session. Group leaders can use these notes to guide the group discussions and keep the group on-track

SESSION ONE

TRAUMA

Question #4 — There are a wide variety of causes from emotional distress, a few include:

1. Divorce

2. Auto collisions

3. Sudden death of family/ friend

4. Sudden Illness

5. Financial issues

6. Witnessing any traumatic event

Question #5 — Some ways people avoid the pain of a broken heart include:

1. Isolation

2. Become angry and bitter — blame others

3. Use mind altering substances

4. Make inner vows

5. Judge their offender — blame them

6. Try harder to please others

Question #6 -- Some somatic illnesses include:

1. Muscle aches

2. Headache

3. High blood pressure

4. Depression

5. Auto-immune disease

6. Diabetes

Question # 7 — Many behaviors can develop via generational sin due to trauma, some include:

1. Alcoholism

2. Child abuse

3. Abandonment

4. Racism

5. Drug abuse

6. Spousal abuse

SESSION TWO

UNDERSTANDING THE BIBLE

Question #3 — Open discussion

Question #4 — Consequences of Adam's sin are:

1. Spiritual then physical death

2. Loss of fellowship with God

3. All descendants are now born in sin

4. Child birth would now be a painful event

5. The ground of the earth was cursed — man was to now have hard labor obtaining food

6. Shame and blame entered into the world

7. A blood sacrifice was now required to atone for sin

8. Adam and Eve were ejected from the Garden of Eden

9. All women will want to rule over their husbands

Question #5 — God's attributes include:

1. God is omnipotent — all powerful

2. God is omniscient — all knowing

3. God is omnipresent — He is everywhere at the same time

4. God is our healer

5. God is love

Question #6 — Open discussion

Question #7 — Being conformed to this world means to behave in a fleshly manner which includes :

1. Idolatry

2. Immorality

3. Being envious

4. Arguing

5. Jealousy

6. Racism

SESSION THREE

SURRENDERING TO GOD'S AUTHORITY

Question #3 — Open discussion

Question #4 — Open discussion

Question #5 — Open discussion

SESSION FOUR

THE KEY ROLE OF SALVATION

Question #3 — Grace is defined as:

1. Undeserved or unmerited favor

2. God's gift of grace is not based on anything that we have done — we are undeserving of His love and mercy — it is all about God.

Question #4 — Open discussion

Question #5 — Some of the things we can do to help our sanctification include:

1. Study the bible

2. Go to church

3. Listen to sermons - church — radio

4. Fellowship with other Christians

5. Forgive others

6. Walk in the Holy Spirit

SESSION FIVE

MEANING OF THE VIRGIN BIRTH

Reading the scriptures and open discussion

SESSION SIX

SIN

Question #3 — When we sin, we simply confess the sin to God and repent (make an effort to turn away from the sin) and God will forgive us for that sin. Our relationship with God is restored and we are considered righteous.

Walking in darkness is being disobedient to God and not following His will.

Question #4 — There are many consequences to sin, some include:

1. Emotional distress

2. Depression

3. Unable to find peace

4. Illness

5. Loss of joy

6. Sin has generational consequences

Without acknowledging our sin through confession and repentance, we remain in habitual sin. Sin causes havoc in our lives, prevents a close relationship with God, and blocks healing.

SESSION SEVEN

WHO YOU ARE IN CHRIST

Read all listed scripture and discuss with the group

SESSION EIGHT

WHY GOD ALLOWS SUFFERING

Read the listed scriptures and discuss with the group

SESSION NINE

OBSTACLES TO HEALING

Question #3 — Group discussion

Question #4 -- Group discussion

Question #5 -- Group discussion

Question #6 -- Group discussion

Question #7 -- We can defeat the Law of Diminishing Returns by listening and obeying the Holy Spirit's prompting when we sin. The conviction of the Holy Spirit should bring us to repentance. If we ignore the Holy Spirit's voice, we remain in habitual sin that keeps us separated from God that causes us emotional distress and blocks our healing.

Question #8 — This is a very difficult question to answer. Everyone's definition of "honor" is different. I believe what it means to follow this commandment includes:

1. Forgiving your parent(s).

2. Thank them for the things that they have done for you.

3. Reconciliation is not required, however, forgiveness is the first step to reconciliation.

4. Consider that your parent(s) may have been abused in a similar manner when they were young. This generational sin is being handed down. Meet with them and ask. Tell them how you feel, if they deny what happened or do not acknowledge your feelings, you have at least fulfilled God's will.

SESSION TEN

FORGIVENESS

Question #3 — Our strength is through Jesus Christ. The faith we have that Jesus will provide us with that strength comes from bible study, knowing who God is, who Jesus is, and what He has done for us. The strength we have in Jesus Christ gives us the power to overcome all obstacles.

Question #4 — Jesus teaches that we must forgive our offender 490 times. This really means that we must forgive EVERY time. Forgiveness is not to let our offender off the hook, but it is to release the excess baggage we carry because of it. Jesus knows the damage that unforgiveness causes. There is no healing without forgiveness.

SESSION ELEVEN

CONFESSION AND REPENTANCE

Question #3 — Group discussion — Everyone should confess and repent as soon as possible to prevent a calloused conscience

Question #4 -- Group discussion

Question #5 — Group discussion

SESSION TWELVE

PRAYER

Question #3 — Prayer should be our first response to any and all situations. We are not to rely on our own ability to make good decisions and respond properly to difficult situations. We are to depend on God.

Question #4 -- Group discussion

Question #5 — We can get to know God's will better by:

1. Study the bible

2. Listen to sermons

3. Fellowship with Christians

4. Go to church

5. Serve others

6. Walk in the Holy Spirit

NOTES

NOTES

NOTES

NOTES

NOTES

NOTES

NOTES

NOTES

NOTES

NOTES

NOTES

NOTES

NOTES

NOTES

NOTES

NOTES

NOTES

NOTES

NOTES

NOTES

www.ingramcontent.com/pod-product-compliance
Lightning Source LLC
Chambersburg PA
CBHW060244030426
42335CB00014B/1595